J
599.755
JOH   Johnson, Jinny

Leopard

DUE DATE

busy baby animals

leopard

Please visit our web site at: www.garethstevens.com
For a free color catalog describing Gareth Stevens' list of high-quality books
and multimedia programs, call 1-800-542-2595 (USA) or 1-800-461-9120 (Canada).
Gareth Stevens Publishing's Fax: (414) 332-3567.

Library of Congress Cataloging-in-Publication Data

Johnson, Jinny.
  Leopard / by Jinny Johnson; [illustrated by Ch'en-Ling; photography by Susanna Price].
  —North American ed.
    p. cm — (Busy baby animals)
  ISBN 0-8368-2927-1 (lib. bdg.)
    1. Leopard—Infancy—Juvenile literature. [1. Leopard. 2. Animals—Infancy.]
  I. Ch'en-Ling, ill. II. Price, Susanna, ill. III. Title.
  QL737.C23J618   2001
  599.75'54139—dc21   2001020528

This North American edition first published in 2001 by
Gareth Stevens Publishing
A World Almanac Education Group Company
330 West Olive Street, Suite 100
Milwaukee, Wisconsin 53212 USA

This U.S. edition © 2001 by Gareth Stevens, Inc. Original edition © 2000 by
Marshall Editions Developments Ltd. First published by Marshall Publishing Ltd.,
London, England.

Illustrations: Ch'en-Ling
Photography: Susanna Price
Editor: Elise See Tai
Designer: Caroline Sangster
Gareth Stevens editor: Katherine J. Meitner
Gareth Stevens cover design: Katherine A. Kroll

Printed in the United States of America

1 2 3 4 5 6 7 8 9 05 04 03 02 01

leopard

Jinny Johnson

Gareth Stevens Publishing
A WORLD ALMANAC EDUCATION GROUP COMPANY

When Nibu was born, he stayed hidden with his sisters in their safe, warm den. The litter of cubs grew quickly, drinking their mother's milk.

Now Nibu leaves the den and goes outside to play. He is very curious, so he sniffs and paws everything he sees.

Leopards are good climbers. Nibu tries to follow his mother up a tree, but he is not quite strong enough yet.

Nibu and his sisters like to wrestle and pounce on top of each other. Playful fighting helps young leopards grow strong and practice their hunting skills.

When they are tired, the cubs lick each other clean before they go to sleep.

Leopards
sleep during
the day and
hunt at night.

13

Nibu's mother is out hunting. Someday, Nibu will be a hunter, too. But, for now, he waits for his mother to return. She'll be back soon, Nibu.

More about Leopards

Leopards are members of the cat family. They live in Africa and Asia and can survive in many different habitats, from deserts to rain forests. These powerful predators hunt all kinds of prey, including birds, snakes, other mammals, and even insects. Leopards are usually active at night, but they will hunt during the day in areas where they are not disturbed by humans. Leopards live alone and come together only for mating. A female has one to four cubs at a time. The cubs stay with her for about eighteen months. Male leopards do not help females raise the cubs.